Niall McDevitt

b/w

First published in 2010
by Waterloo Press (Hove)
95 Wick Hall
Furze Hill
Hove BN3 1PF

Printed in Palatino 10.7pt by
One Digital
Unit 7 Woodingdean Business Park,
Sea View Way, Brighton BN2 6NX

Reprinted (2022) in honour of Cordi Murphy,
from one bohemian to another.

A CIP record for this book is available
from the British Library

ISBN 978-1-906742-11-9

Acknowledgements

Some of these poems were published in *The London Magazine, New Departures, UP!, Off, Rising, Poems on the Buses, Openned*. Many were published in *The Wolf*. Others have been broadcast on *The Verb, Home Truths, Bespoken Word* and Resonance 104.4FM. 'Off-Duty' won *The Verb* Urban Poetry Competition 2005.

Of many to thank, I name James Byrne and John O'Donoghue.

Contents

3

4

Poetry: Tok we oli raetem blong narafala man i ridim blong kasem
   stret tingting we man we i raetem i stap harem long hat blong hem.

(Talk where all he write him belong another fellow man
he read him belong catch him straight think think where man
where he write him he stop hear him along heart belong him)

A New Bislama Dictionary (ed. Terry Crowley)

In memory of Ken Campbell
'Bigfala Jif'

1941-2008

b/w

1

… But now behold
In the quick forge and working-house of thought
How London doth pour out her citizens.

Shakespeare

THE ICON
for Sophia

this fury and sorrow
is of the icon
emanating from the icon

who works for pharaohs
is seen in falcons
and carvings of falcons

there is no tomorrow
for man or woman
but in the woman

who in her burrow
a mind is making
an intelligence is making

as bow-and-arrow
its target is seeking
its tip is seeking

to pierce the marrow
of the living token
and the dying token

the falcon is furrowed
its god is forsaken
its cosmology is forsaken

for ones and zeros
the images are broken
the icon is broken

ELIZABETH 43

1

    of the rough youth
    and conception
    how fresh in the dirt
    the poor kept turning through the turnstiles

no ease of being in dirt of streets
                   as were

              whom her 'p' penalized

                      things
                     turn
    the mad the poor and whoever we were
    never decrease in number
    but you must live
    in your own adventure
    and the new kings will come
    to
    how adventurous to be

2

                      policed by
alcohol crowds
things in times of
a care
      not in

    but the new lights of the new seasons
    flood the public spaces
    high above high towers
    and the transcendental carts

below
a king   to be

        burning

3

this dole an Elizabeth
now I'd friendly be
with the fire-people   in the palindrome
                                         (not knowing
what it is to turn on a neolithic wheel
come crossed into the light of the examiners)
I'd globe my head
cup it in cups to see the suns
                                              in it

          amid the rough banter
          no one is a part of
          or the town-crier hysteria

competing to be allowed to be in light
how you'd wish to live could choose:

                    the workhouse
          rain-drinkers   rain

4

sticking to historybook rules   tablet rules

we israelites   learning how
                          how the thing is
nothing new
which made its laws to run
biblically
                                        in fold   in pen
               the humans of *Numbers*
none
                          small

[Author's note: the 43rd Elizabeth is also known as the Elizabethan Poor
Law, a 'Relief Act' of 1601]

HORSESHOES
i.m. Michael Hartnett (1941-1999)

> *Praise from the apprentice is always shown*
> *in miniatures of a similar stone*

1
Hammersmith Broadway:
a cauldron of emissions,
   a CO_2 stew.

2
River of two tides
flows to the west and east, rides
   red-green in ebbings.

3
The old... Grey, silver,
white. Mobility scooters,
   zimmer frames. Moving...

4
In *Tesco Metro*,
bargain hunter-gatherers.
   Paleolithic.

5
An Irishman stops,
fucked as me on a bad day,
   talks of Donaghy.

6
Ambulances cry
—in the darkness, in the light—
   a song of spirals.

7
Hearses and roses
black and red by Augustine's.
   The grim chauffeurs smoke.

8
Here, Isis is God,
Thames hunting in the hare moon,
  a magic anvil.

9
A flock of ferals
statuesque on the roof-tops...
  Blacks Road is silent.

10
A granite Shakespeare
idles at the library.
  Jets boomerang west.

11
The Plough and Harrow.
Ancient men nickname it
  'the departure lounge'.

12
ARK in its mooring
by the A4 flyover.
  Fumes flood the levels.

13
Margravine Gardens
is red in sun. The dead's dusk
  is sweet as living's.

14
Cormorants on Thames
—wing-waving in ritual—
  hook the opaque foams.

15
Policemen on mounts.
Horseshoes clang in Hammersmith.
  Echolalia.

THE JEWESS
after Modigliani

> *à la cime argentée je reconnus la déesse*

in the freedom of the trees a Jewess comes to rope
me
to arks of red and blue and green
warning of dangers rains masochisms
things dragged by horse-sense
fire and neurosis
to which she must cede control
bled from the Matronit
red from the Shekhinah
escaping to her Red Sea
(why lie on her
if not her equal
or lie about her?)
whom none crawl like
on the grape-rich continents
her own tree uprooting
Africa to Europe to Britain
come to the honeycomb
of Goldsmiths
cutting diamonds with her 'paste is paste' teeth
that are the invisible teeth of birds
so hooded
so hooked
is she
flying in the storms of the New Middle Ages
above citadels
calling in taxes
and labour of the tall Bulgarians etc.
who answer to her red shields

I answered to her
was taxed—being stiffnecked—
by the voice of a falcon testing its own force
lifting from black level upto/into gold wasserfalls
was privy to a female concert
(eggs come) (blood falls)

mystified by more than meets eyes or penis or hands
moving in kitchens
even
who has surveyed the 20th century
and says: 'Fassbinder is spectacular artist'
who non-believer
sees the human afterlife as that of 'fertilizer'
is ideas-woman
                    fall-woman
                                parchment-woman
                                            screen-woman
full using her claws to land and study...

and is she from Kedron or Negev—though Athenian—
debarred from holy mountain
in a dream that did not end so well of
fathering/daughtering her loss of patriarch?
the child in photos looking like Anne Frank
eyes globed and graced—such gems!—
now with absolute instinct for threat and survival
in
say a dangerous mission through a forest of landlords
has come politically environmentally aesthetically correct
jettisoning the platonic for the new jargons
discounting the theft of sparks by gnostic
                                shoplifters

in sparks of gnostics I come to her honouring
with Hildegard and the hordes
of Sophiologists
who own the magpie
who claw for gems
is her own gem
and lines and bruises
(the purpleyellow fruits of her jaffa aura)
clustering
round her weird smile

eggs fall
blood comes

TO A LION-SKIN RUG
for Palash

Does a lion think? Not of ending its days in a stately home
as a trophy at the top of the staircase, two-dimensional,
the bulk scavenged off to a light-brown, flat, floppy pancake
draped in an archway, a nothing in lion's clothing;
no leonine tools of the trade, no *Coeur de Lion* pumping
the blood of a Richard to flex his claws on Saracen sands,
dead to the world, a mini-desert with a hairy dune:
the deaths-head (twisted up to seem it's still roaring

but looking like it suffers from a neck disorder called torticollis);
… really just a pussycat, safe for an Aesopian mouse
to play in the jaws or tiptoe along the whiskers,
debate with dull orange eyes from a position of strength
and out-squeal the uber-miaow, out-scuttle the loping stride
of the golden killer who can't even manage a bowl
of *Kit-e-Kat*. Is it thinking now? Not of chicken liver chunkies
but dreaming of Sekhmet, her womanly hips and breasts,
                                                    her cobra.

[Author's note: Sekhmet is the Egyptian goddess of war, woman with lion head, star of the Egyptian Room at the British Museum.]

SONG OF THE JINN

And of those demons that are found
In fire, air, flood, or underground
Milton

We created the jinn from the fire of hot wind
From the tips of flames, not from clay
The Evil Eye crosses the Sirat, blind
We created the jinn from the fire of hot wind
The head of the sleeper with knots they bind
Some are righteous, some He's led astray
We created the jinn from the fire of hot wind
From the tips of flames, not from clay

Who was the first to call *Isha* 'darkness'?
Shaytan who walks with one sandal
Far out in the sea is the throne of Iblis
Who was the first to call *Isha* 'darkness'?
Who would not prostrate? Who was proud and faithless?
Who was arrogant among all angels?
Who was the first to call *Isha* 'darkness'?
Shaytan who walks with one sandal

The jinn—like men—die till the Day of Rising
Not of dust, they will not be scattered
In the Time of Ignorance, Al-Uzza (the shaytan)
The jinn—like men—die till the Day of Rising
Obedient only to charms and to talismans
Come Ramadan, dark spirits are fettered
The jinn—like men—die till the Day of Rising
Not of dust, they will not be scattered

Jinn: genies (sing. *jinni*) spirits lower than angels who can take human or
animal shape and having a supernatural power over humans
Sirat: knife-edged bridge leading to the Garden
Shaytan: Satan or an evil genie
Iblis: Satan's proper name (as in diabolis)
Al-Uzza: tree worshipped in pagan times but really just a genie in disguise

BLUE SELF-EXISTING NIGHT

the lines in their courses
moving to move through
this black/white doubt

walking in blue smog
ice binds the veins
and intrigue of friends

firm are the churches
first of the gothic
stalwart in their carvings

who colds the crypts though?
who colds the squares?
hope coils to warm

cranes cross blue shades
scope the towers thin
with zigzag possibilities

running to the signs
John rechecks the names
elfing his way

buses move as buildings
hum-humming in Venice
upriver in a glide

the new stars scraping
items of cutlery
in a velvet case

realms out of corners
booths on the borders
to telephone through dreams:

'hey! she's been decoded,
is amused with it…
Blue Self-Existing Night
is now her name'

in boulevards and tubes
of the bomb-scared streets
busy hips are flexing

BABEL

of the news in England of England in English delivered in English
  accents
I am fly-on-the-wall impotent to but listen to the received
  pronunciations of it
and know that I am in mid-Jihad and be suspicious of every syllable
that issues forth from newsreaders politicians and professional-all-
  too-professional lips
and I'm pissed off with media accents because in England most of
  them are English
(though in Ireland—strangely—I didn't give a flying that all of
  them were Irish)
and whenever you hear an accent on English airwaves that isn't
  English,
it jars (usually Paddy/Jock/Taff or American/Afro-Caribbean/Asian
  or Northern
English heh!) and stinks of tokenism and you feel sorry for the
  non-English accent
in its brief allotted slot and immediately wish for the English accents
  to come back
(which they do) and now since the Jihad took off you can't turn on
  the radio
without being flooded by tidal waves of loquacious Muslim
  spokespeople
and my crapped-out paranoid history-warped baked-potato-with-
  beans of a mind
thinks: 'England is buttering up the Muslims by giving them lots of
  publicity
by interviewing them all the time about mosques Koran hijabs
  Ramadan halal
and generally making them feel included, listened to, important,
  nice, not all terrorists
etc. (even while the police are shooting innocent Muslims in their
  homes)'
and then my crapped-out paranoid media-warped fried-steak-and-
  frites of a mind
thinks: 'but in the time of the Irish Jihad there was not the slightest
  attempt

by the British Brainwashing Corporation to butter up the Irish
    community
and—Wogan apart—make them feel like fellow citizens, nice, not
    all terrorists etc.'

when the Real I.R.A. planted a bomb on Hammersmith Bridge in
    the year 2000
no one interviewed me about *Ulysses* Guinness folk-songs Heaney
    and/or Tayto crisps
adding: 'oh and by the way we're 100% convinced you had
    nothing to do with it'

(you don't have to be a mind-reader to read the mind of England)

there is a serious problem with the English media and with accents
    generally
and we should be looking into and discussing and debating the
    abolition of accents
and everyone should have their own unique customized accent
    like an identity card
and RP is not neutral but a Southern bourgeois accent / accents are
    a thing of the past
and in the cities is a human sound-collage that's never reflected
    replayed represented
in an English media that for some reason keeps on hiring 99%
    English accents
(not that I mind if it's Ken Campbell Jeremy Hardy or the
    dreamlike Charlotte Green
and while we're at it the lack of Birmingham accents on the air is
    a national scandal)
and so my friends the only solution is to tune into the Radio Babel
    of the streets:
the shopkeepers/drinkers/employed/unemployed/children/Moors
    and endless French

[Author's note: the other solution is to tune into Resonance 104.4fm – via
internet if you're outside London…]

THE ENEMY

In abundance of iniquity, many loves wax cold

                                          Christ

I/we/you/they
            turn to enemy:

microbes chew the teeth
in nights in winds
in time of the breaking of hymens
in the infamous dens
with the infamous denizens
a judgment from's guts
the dirty man of Europe
loin to loin
and knee

    a humpty-dumpty 'fuck you' officialdom

    'a cry for more money by MI5'

    God's fingerprint on things

    2
        1
            0

    I would have you believe that you're a scoundrel
    an impostor

    here's my card

    I eat on you

    I shit doubt

HISTORY

We are all nobodies in fancy dress:
Caesars, Boadiceas, Napoleons.

Is it the Black Death or is it Bad Faith?
To feel is to be infected.

I cannot go naked in history's fields.
I am clad in the body of my father

CAROLINE HOUSE

yesterday I was washerwoman   today I am eggwoman

I run these errands in the equatorial sun—as the parakeets squeak,
as the jeeps rumble—and to me they are heroic   their exhaustion
is wine

light bakes the scalp on these pollen-rich streets   we walk through
yellow fall-out, shoes touching the cauldron

though I'm not shaped as a goddess 8 and don't carry baskets
on my crown, my chores are primal and my days are danced...
at night, a crown of stars fixes onto my forehead

Caroline House is my seat, my canopy-of-estate   it's near the river
(in the air is the tang of river-salt)

spraying the mahogany with wood-polish, I saw Azrael in the sheen
(he spoke to me from the sheen)

my mother lives in Elizabeth House   30 years divide us
she is my mentor

and into this realm I usher more daughters   oh the square miles
of space: Sophia House, Eleanor House, Beatrice House

tomorrow I'll be needlewoman

the lift is out-of-order

we walk the flights, with Caroline

[Author's note: The Queen Caroline Estate, Hammersmith, is named after
Caroline of Brunswick who lived in Hammersmith during the coronation of
her estranged husband King George IV, soon after which she was murdered.
Each of the houses in the estate is named after a different queen of England.]

CONDOM

They have my surname
—Those jelly corpses
In that body bag—
But no first names
Whom the mystery would not usher
Through the latex veil

  The kings who never touched an evil land
  The gamblers who never saw a horse-race
  The feminists who lived their lives
  In the centre of a testicle
  Characters who never amounted to much
  (a teaspoon of death)
  Their heartbreaks and salvations
  In the subjunctive countries
  Epic
  But black-and-white

  Catholics?
  They are doves
  In a halo

    the b/w film in which I and you
    and all the living are pooled
    climaxes again at dawn
    bursting into coloured balls

THE DRUM

Let them make my skin into drum-heads for the Bohemian cause
                                                        Jan Zizak

We have drummed the millennium, out-there, cultic, weird,
In the noumenal city of sha-manic cabaret,
In blue face-paint, black face-paint, bird-claws, robes and shrouds,
                                        John Crow/Niall Dubh etc.
In shoes that tap-danced the boards of the true theatre:
The TAZ, the Temple of Thespis, the Drunken Boat,
                                        Temporary Autonomous Zone
The floating pirate utopia whose burgundy decks
—slanted—were impossible to walk when sober
For the cut-throats and their fungi mundi cargoes:
                                        Shrooms of the Universe
(Hakim, the wise man, our cachinnating figure head)
                                        Hakim Bey (CIA?)
(Mongrel, the moon-faced, ranting from his dog-wild abdomen)
Rave strobes to navigate the black cavernous gulf,
Treasure maps and sea-scrolls charting the anti-trade routes
To the last ungoverned, unpoliced clods of earth
In the fizgig interzones of these our Left-Hand Islands.
                                        Ex-British Isles
Customised illnesses we carried on our backs
Absconding from the fatal state-approved leisure dome,
Invading the Drome of the shape-shifters, time travellers,
Goblin hordes in the skunk-perfumed dust tunnels,
The Elfin Crew (glimmering eyes made of conjuration).
All spaces were sacred, all rituals were site-specific
Where the wild children lived and laboured…
At Cathedral, Satan strapped on her red-hot dildo.
At Globe, our Christ-on-a-Bike drank Tennents Super.
'Twas a sex-organic hot-tub rebirthing in the time-space womb
For the mad families of Chaos Gaia Eros
Who once were disconnected in the Mordoresque dark
Of the all-pervasive brainwash: mediation.

Land animals we became, lords of the air.
Jesus complexes swooped, abseiled, parachuted
Into the leper temples for rites libations
And much public healing of the body anarchic.
Sha-manic clinics, multiversities, moral brothels
(deregulated) were established and disestablished
To the deranged laughter of the health-and-safety inspectors.
Others fed the monster: BALOR. We fed the grid.

Celtic Cyclops

Stallholders sold the nectars: iboga / peyote / salvia.
Players gyrated in paleolithic penis-gourds

The Pidgin Players

Lost in a glossolalia of Queen's and Pidgin English,
Captain World in his trickster's helmet—a wolfskin headdress—
Inciting us to haka-summon the ancestor spirits.
Everyone was infamous, blacklisted, deathlisted
For being sworn to the ECO-TORT, the duty of care.
'Twas insufficient to see it with your own two eyes,
Only Eye 3 could apprehend the colour-bombs,
The fulgurations, the fireballs, the orbs of night,
The self-transforming elves, the hyper-spaceships
And the ear was the eye that saw the piped music.
'War on all muzak!' was the logos of the drum
As the numbers spun on time's axis: 99... 00... 01
Genius was collective. Genie? Us...
We turned the islands upside-down for justice.
Drum was the rule, drum was the politics

Rhythms of Resistance

And in all minds was hung a drum-skin of goat
And in all hands was a witchdoctor's stick:
Brotherhood of the bodhran,
Sisterhood of the singing-bowl

GEORGE ORWELL IS FOLLOWING ME

in *the moon under water*
he's slumped at my table with a bargain bitter
heavily disguised as a member of the proletariat

george orwell is invigilating my existence
in the bleak streets and bombsites
I feel the force of his eyes
from where he stands tall thin intent as a surveillance camera

george orwell is insidious and ubiquitous
in one of the bookshops of obfuscation
he was stocktaking on a metallic ladder
false moustache (over his own tory anarchist moustache)

orwell is always busy on the next bowl
of the public urinals
sniffing his piss-steam with scientific disgust
and debating the merits of the henry millers

the most remarkable people turn out to be orwells
I threw a couple of twopenny coins
to an old etonian in a cardboard box
who said: 'what do you do in this shithole with five pence?'

at night when I've made it to my safehouse
again the whirring of lenses
and he's standing over my bed with a birch
keeping me awake (i.e. protecting me from sleep)

george orwell is following me
in the *wetherspoons* boozer
he's slumped at my table with a bargain bitter
heavily disguised as a member of the underclass

LIBERTY CAPS
for John Crow

And hooded with knowledge,
nippled bells for heads,
the diminutive druids
make their white assembly.
Another year is annulled
from textbooks of history.
Faces twist and glower
in the incandescent grass
of these elfin initiates
empowered with highest gifts;
(behind the hood the glint).
Tacit the warlock armies
reconvening on the hilltops
whose lore is excluded
from scripts of history.
We merely guess at the myths
of their war against war;
and again on left-hand islands
—summoned by rain like blood
drumming into the earth—
white wands, white arrows
point into dark-age minds,
more ancient than our
philosophy or agriculture,
for the newborn to feed on
the nipple-milk of wonder.

MEMORIES OF A SIX MONTH RELATIONSHIP

1

your face on pillows
bird-like mole-like (profiled in mornings)
always
more than woman

2

your delight in the white flowers
of a jasmine plant
sparking from green vines

white life in winter

3

the image of you
in your own painting
'lost weekend'
shadow of a ragdoll
hunched as if on strings
abstracted from the form
(the form
of you)
an idea of Plato

4

the atmosphere of intelligence
playing about your face
a super-consciousness
never off / always on
really
an extra light

5

corvine… a creature in black
discernible in shopping aisles
subtly gothic
Kafka's sister
clayey ears
growths pointed and monstrous
betraying your Golem origins
hidden in black hair…
the sister of Kafka!

6

you at your desk computing
or building a spliff
head bird-shaped in concentration
(the Owl of Athens)

7

your download of songs
with its recurring blasts of
The Band of Holy Joy
and the holy joy I felt sometimes
in your holy room, New Cross

8

black silk red stripes
of your kung fu pants
femininity circling the masculinity
(of you of me)
twirling kicks / shadow punches
on the grass at Goldsmiths

9

in the gothic interior
of the Montague Arms
with its weird stucco
like a horrible fungus
pirate ship / cathedral
—you in supernatural habitat—
ah! those hallowed marijuana-enhanced beers
pulled
by the gargoyle maids

10

the menagerie in you:
crow / scorpion / bat etc.
your soul a zoo…
the way you'd shout in that Gonzo voice
Owl of Athens
always more than human

Epilogue (23.23pm)

a text from you:
'the orchids are dying
and I am very sad xx'

TO THE INTELLECTUAL PROPRIETORS

To the blimps, farts, nobs and twits,
The would-be colonialists of poetry:
Why not stop pretending to be literary
And let go of your illusions, your elites?

To the pseuds, sharks, squares and shits
Who buy and sell intellectual property
As if there were no such thing as poverty
And Thoreau and co. never lived in it…

To the pricks, cunts, glandes and clits
Who 'sex up' the same old mediocrity
For a bourgeois / PC / moral majority:
History *will* consign you to plague pits.

[Author's note: 'glandes' is the plural of glans]

IN LONDON
after 'In Jerusalem' by Mahmoud Darwish

In London, within the crumbs and shards of Roman wall,
I walk from epoch to epoch, a tour-guide, stumbling
into the black-and-white facade of Tudorbethan houses.
Below street-level—in an underground car-park—
is one of the 'holy of holies'. Its chancel extends eons.
Here, an invisible street, Shakespeare rose. (Humans rise.
How? They work and play in a theme-park called Eden).
Outside is a huge chunk of London Wall, with steps,
like a Greek amphitheatre. Nearby is a herb garden,
with tangles of mandrake, next to Barber-Surgeons Hall.
There were handfastings in this quarter, much adultery,
and on Ascension Day things really began to take off...

I pulled white roses, walked Milk Street to Silver Street
among Marranos and Huguenots, talking in honeyed English,
looking into the hearts of the people I lived with, a poetic
piss-doctor. I found that with a mere flourish of the quill
I could transfigure lives, gild the human agon. My clients
even called me 'Master'. Some complained of wars,
plagues, fires, floods, but took the incarnations I offered.
The queen died slowly. Then my brother. Then I too exited
as she 'the thousand'
      she the shadow-swan
          played on.

In an underground car-park, I pray for the whale we're in
who ride the British Hieroglyphick, strangers here.

b/w

> *And I am black but O my soul is white*
> Blake

1 'Adam' (sol niger)

the cinemascope of Tamesis
screens a millionfold images
Celtic/Roman/Saxon
in her time-space mirror
> but no one
> was born
> to the river
> as Adam

a
> *boy seen in the blue-grey expanse*
> *London looking on London*
> *(through a glass darkly)*
> *ten days after 9/11*

a
> *relic of himself*

a
> *torso in orange shorts*

a
> *potion of clay*
> *and gold in his belly*
> *as the LATE PRICES EXTRA*
> *banners were being written*

for the abstract: money

(ating se magie noire i stap long background)

duty-bound to the barrier

pure

the river held him up like Isis
her brother
in the medicinal limb-growing sun
and he was remembered
disfala lilfala
blak riva i swimswim
no han no fut
i go long bigsi

2 Blong Blakman

Tok ia—pijin—i tok blong blakman.
Olsem wanem waetman ia i yusum?
Waetman ia i afsaed, i aninit,
i slev? Naoia niufala tok i jusum?

Lanwis blong blakman i lanwis blong wol

Mi mi no stap long kantri blong mi.
Mi mi no save spik lanwis blong mi.
Sipos mi toktok wetem tang blong waetman
Mi mi no save talem fulwan stori.

Lanwis blong blakman i lanwis blong wol

Yumifala olgeta i olsem blakman
we yumi wokem long slev plantesen.
Nem blong plantesen ia i *mani*:
waet suga… waet masta… blak nesen.

Lanwis blong blakman i lanwis blong wol

2

In Regions of Humanity, in Londons opening streets...

Blake

A NIGHT IN WITH ROGET

Caesarism, Kaiserism, Czarism…

these seem otherworldly to me
in my bird-box consulting Roget
as a zero-drop in temperature
hits the nerve system of millions.
(Even my lioness turns frigid).
There's no adjusting it, no controlling
this zenith to nadir blood.

Melancholia, blues, blue devils...

lazars sign the visitor-book,
Son of Man eyes, blue conflagrations,
winters and summers spinning.
There's no cure but work, love,
new jackets, false teeth, meetings,
cheap wine.
                Where do we begin?
This blue-on-blue is impossible.

Genesis, Origin, Provenance…

white flakes are falling.

Creator, Preserver, Demiurge…

how do we 'out-Herod Herod'?

NOTES FROM WETHERSPOON
(The Plough and Harrow, King Street, Hammersmith)

for Christopher Twigg

A pub on this site since 1419, I'm grogged
      on the medieval energy,

a yeasted serf. A pub on this site for the
      children of the death,

a nut-brown ale is the jab, the inoculation,
      of their redding veins.

Here the Chaucerians douse their comedies
      in cap-and-bells draughts

for a farting surplus and a poxing mouth
      with the grimmer Langlandians.

The sups are choral, the jibes and jests
      a ribbiting of bullfrogs

bulging brown and green in these holy fens
      where Sin and Death

growl a low glossolalia no one can fathom,
      ears clogged with mead.

Here I turn from a technocratic city-state
      back to the plough

via the time-machine of a glass vessel
      cutting with starry edges.

I ride the fabliaux, rein in ribald tales
      to a barleycorn music

as Hunt and Holst look from the walls
        on we motley mortals

in our art village, in our artisan hamlet
        rung with its forges

to a belled, visionary 'Field of Folk' idyll
        pacific as the shire-horse.

A pub on this site since 1419, I toast
        the taxman who cometh.

THE NETHERWORLD HOTEL
for the international caramel children

1

Kamil, the vampiric night-porter, is connecting the switchboard calls.
Is it merely the night work which makes him so pale?
Many have speculated on his vices and failed to pinpoint them.
He has sat in counsel with Mr. Rosenberg the proprietor
—forceful, subtle, fallacious, proving his innocence—
(little Nugent the manager acting as witness)
and fascinated the proprietor as no other employee had for years.
Yet the pallor hangs about his Egyptian head: an inverse halo of guilt.
His knife-like nose and chin are observable from the outside streets
gouging about in the television screen window.
His eyes, most of all, seem always to be unsheathed.
He has seen it all and sold it all: opium, logic, magic.
Kamil—the genie—arranges everything for the accredited guests
from room-keys to nocturnal appointments with Mrs. Wong
and leads them deeper into the fog than they will ever notice
(for the fog is not noticeable close up).

2

No one complains about the rooms in *The Netherworld Hotel*
or the fact that they use bricks for ash-trays.
To do so would be laughter-inducing, legendary.
The bill from the constant use of the dry-ice machines must be
    astronomical
but the extravagance covers up cracks, cockroaches, burns, damp,
as well as lending the classic 'crematorium atmosphere'
that always brings the old users scooting their scooters back
and has the new ones kneeling at the red door, conferring,
when they turn up after-hours to a neon NO VACANCIES,
the hotel itself sucking on their disappointment
as if chasing the dragon down the moonlit tinfoil steps.

3

After an undisclosed period of residence at *The Netherworld*
you become a phantom and no longer need a soft bed.
The night-porter will sell your passport to Algerian contacts
and you too will profit

(pure puff)

4

then float on deadsea memories of opium clouds insect orchestras
lotus girls incommunicado vanishing into fog blankets looking-glasses
red velvet curtains infested with a connoisseur's a collector's moths
dilapidated conference rooms where seekers queued for robed gurus
monks pimps sailors gleemen known to the malodorous corridors
hashashins equipped with hookahs and theories of the 'neural synapses'
chambermaids in blue-flower uniforms of beauty and tooth-decay
Jesus—the barman—mustachioed who originally hails from Madrid
zigzag basement rooms where we hid from parental bloods and wills

opium coda

opium boredom
regale me (again)
with tales of a Chinese incarnation
(oui moi le Chinois!)
concubine poppies
and the evil karma
zen-eyed whorling
on that 4th century pillared bed
dreaming right-royal
right-imperial

THE LOFT
in memoriam Tony Jackson

yes I was your friend though I did not know you
in all your rabbinical modes
silver Dylan... most musical of men
in the top room of the pink house

that was the loft of the sages and elders
how was it—hard-won and hard-lost—
they could be both Edenic and sardonic
in the northern-lit swathes of green smoke?

Horovitz Reed Michell et al
passing upto the plateau via the giant steps
memories of Fainlight circle-lining
beyond voltage and mortgage

Su Rose Claudia Egypt and the Alberys
ideas ranged like fresh bread in wooden bowls
a stock exchange of intelligence
free-trading in the cranio-sacral zone

once on the steps myself pouring St. Emilion
under the gold flecks thrown by a Tomlin lamp
Reed in his beret and red velvet jacket
asking: 'have you read *all* of Ballard?'

Oram Dun Crow and Lady K
amid talk of women who iron their hair
Sheldrake the scientist Purce the singer:
guests of your aura

and you at the piano jamming Blake's 'The Tyger'
this in the time of the fruit-juices
when gnosis was yours—palpable—
man of Israel and India and Albion

yes you are my friend and I do not know you
in the density of the mystery
where the spiritual businessmen and businesswomen
live in blue tents above/below the towers

SINGLE MOTHER
for K

your white hair is something brilliant and life-giving
on these grey streets:
a Milky Way with pink pearls in the centre

I see it from my red-brick observatory
and can no more catch onto it
than I can catch onto the moon
riding the whiteness
out
of occluded dark-matter systems
in a silver space-ship pram

who is dutifully mothering
(in halo of saintliness)
a gifted but special-needs child
no more the 'parasite'
of the popular media
and unpopular MPs
than a baby at a nipple

the cheap pin-on angel brooch you gave me
still adorns my lapel
(though the wings have fallen off)

everyone asks about it and I tell them:
'oh I too am a single mother
this
one of my children'

THE GOLD HOSPITAL

at the soma hour of the gold hospital
tuning into the transfiguration
I claim a plateau bed

nothing to be in an ordinary room
without kidney-machine or catheter
then

then wounds are dragon agents
under lasers
and curable

the intoxications the drugging drips
flooding in as if
first experiences

the killing of pain…
I recognize the doctors, I think,
Drs. Blake Gold and Poppy

the zenith is a most unfriendly diamond-mine
hailing
shitting its disposable jewels

told not to told to told of the—more—confusions
the gossiping rain
and super-atomizations

as if science was the new mysticism was the new rock 'n' roll
and touchings of strings
the only reckoning the only evidence the only ever

the hospital is Byzantine and I am not in
it
now mushroomed in my mud-hours

nor warred nor scarred
nor with alcohol gel
rubbing into my lifeline

radio intelligencers
and the various *lw mw* and *fm* voxes
motor-mouthing to the dusk

index of the pilgrims as in their gold rooms
sounds took on momentum
horsed on morphine clouds

illnesses asked for magic
shone through
the flesh the technology

[Author's note: the grey cruciform building of Charing Cross Hospital, Hammersmith, turns at dusk to a colossal, shimmering gold cross.]

CORVIDS

1. shadow cabinet
                              schwarz parliament of crows
in the raucous woods

                         ferocity of agenda
stab-shocks
              daggering bark
                                        nuanced ids
the shades and bones
     eye-names   (inside)

the voices are axes
                chainsaws
                          drills
     they flying and haggling
                         indignant

                 they   wheeling   and   returning
                              rag-black
     rookery daw-days
     elongated by issues
          foul
          palavers

     brutish
                              predatory
          avaricious

the conference a devilsend
     the noise   an annihilation
                bole-claw
drawl of the leaders
                              savage-black
     in civvies

          we depart the parliament's
               sonic thrust-and-cut
raw reasonings   raw resonatings

          machinists of the wood

[42]

2. caw radio

caw radio>>>pain pang>>>clairaudient commune

grin clicks>>>lined on voltings>>>flak

boning>>>claw-tingling>>>renegading

black ack-ack>>>soot spores>>>cinder-crumbling

jet shade>>>scars>>>shit>>>mange

crow radio>>>in wirings>>>fur transistors

rave shadow>>>newsreels on>>>aeriels

snip snap>>>beaks jabs>>>grubs nips pupas

hacksaw>>>cawflap>>>exoskeletal

chainsaw>>>caw>>>metallic chantings

nib nib>>>coal-cloaked>>>nicks in twigs

        cinders>>>splinters

corvine ordeals>>>fuzz>>>interference

zigzagging>>>down>>>blue nacht

3. dead
after seeing Cocteau's *Orphée* and *La Testament d'Orphée*

a hunched jet bundle
on the green mound
unnatural
as an African carving

forks of the claws
twined and scraggy
gloss-body
blue as death

in shadow and grass-blades
magico-religious
ceremonial
fold of the wings

a leaf in its beak
a souvenir a memento
rust-crinkled
the final clutch of

it pausing to think
in a mid-mud glide
of omens
carrion and fugues

plump and ghoulish
eyes like moonspots
sardonic
smirk of the mask

a glow about it
like an obscure diamond
rings hooks
Orphic jewels

a drone of morticians
flapping and circling
obsequies
rude in procession

radioactive the green
mounds and hillocks
macabre
in the oak-hissing park

UMBRELLAS

through the windows of *The William Morris*, I see them
  mushroom:
golf umbrellas, birdcage umbrellas, spots and stripes umbrellas

a sudden gold explosion and the broadway's a deluge-myth

a tree at the navel of the traffic-island volunteers as public
  umbrella, adores the rain.
its band of refugees scatters with the lightning

oak-leaves and dog-ends sail in the gutters at astonishing speeds

girls run as ballerinas, twirling can-can parasols, smiling in hysteria

a Chinaman cowers under his tartan umbrella, profoundly perturbed.
  a Frenchman
with black Paris dome umbrella is more philosophical

the fashion chains and coffee joints are taking a pounding

the storm is white as a Sophia lace wedding umbrella, with gilded
  frame
and ribs, tassels of electricity

the pub's my ark, William Morris my rabbi, illuminated
  by
  slot-machines

rain pelts the black oyster-shells, encrusting, rolls off as pearls

ABEL AND CAIN
150 years after Baudelaire

1

Race of Abel, dine at the Ritz;
capitalism is such bliss.

Race of Cain, Big Mac and frites;
capitalism takes the…

Race of Abel, your gram of coke
powders the nose of seraphim.

Race of Cain, inject or smoke
your £5 wrap of heroin.

Race of Abel, your haute couture
is so chic, so pleasant.

Race of Cain, your cheap sportswear
brands you 'urban peasant'.

Race of Abel, you're from good stock;
success begets success.

Race of Cain, you breed like dogs
—gratis—on the NHS.

Race of Abel, your fat cat premium
is a tad invidious.

Race of Cain, your £5 minimum
is insulting and injurious.

Race of Abel, money fucks
in its penthouse suite.

Race of Cain, in towerblocks,
poverty sucks its teeth.

2

Race of Abel, fill up your arks.
The flood is coming. Flee!

Race of Cain, your Christ, your Marx
haven't set you free.

Race of Abel, there is one bother:
money can't bribe death.

Race of Cain, kill Big Brother
and distribute his wealth.

BLUE
after Jarman

1

in the blue factory the production of emotion
goes on as before
for the blue sons and the blue daughters
growing into a gnosis

(blue truth, blue death)

and in the blue factory the law of supply/demand
goes on

2

blue voice of the blue magus
captivating and liberating
fills the all
fills the blue hall
with soliloquy and swansong
to drug the disease
of being in transience
with a joy and gravitas
and a play and prayer

I keep going back to hear

3

who fall into the blue zone
bathe in a sky
the colour of amnesia

Susannah Simona Samantha Sophia
turn to blue

4

in the blue cinema I could be transfixed
by blue images of love and death
coming from the colour as from a reservoir
putting things into perspective, yes,
putting things in their places
sheltering in your doorway
as women from rain

TWO POEMS

1. *crack-whore*

she'll strut the grey blur the A to Z jigsaw
and feel the city revolving about her hips
ebon-fleshed clay-glossy cool in their nets
she is
         her own saleswoman and merchandise

the phantoms she's had the 1000 minor officials
of Pluto who come to consult her in shadows
would grope her demon made by silkworms
and rip it to tatters with their cobra fangs

she's sold to black magic her cells need crystal
(just a few rocks to build her own African palace)
as here in the lead-rich labyrinth she commands
skeleton troops to invade
                              drains
                                    gutters
                                         conduits

2. whore's noodles

Chinese as the night—and omnipresent—
she's so flexible she feels immune from death
in these peepshow streets Soho's the globe
the opium-eclipsed moons of her eyes orbit

    neon noodles neon spaghetti
    of Chinatown and Little Italy
    cross-pollination of red sirens red lights
    glowering in the Circean Gulf

    and the shanghaied man shall hang
    from the horny cusp
    as he pays his black widow
    by gold card

         ....

China White—with a pidgin whisper—
disappears behind a DO NOT DISTURB
already she can smell the sea-slugs the sandalwood
chop-chopping as one who is immune from love

THE NETTLES

Yield stinging nettles to mine enemies;
And when they from thy bosom pluck a flower,
Guard it, I pray thee, with a lurking adder

A standing army of witches,
green in the sun,
bony and hideous;

a 1000-strong coven,
dry as dust, lined,
wrinkled and odious;

they snicker in winds,
hexing, gossiping
of henbane and wormwood;

crack-voiced, cantankerous,
silver-webbed crones
twisting for mischief

in inch-plots of earth
and roots to strangle
the innocent maggots;

so arid, so wizened,
faces like scabbards
to lunge and to slit

with spells and curses;
all's pinched, all's shrivelled;
no rain could revive

these wisps of ill-nature
with a benediction
whom bells make titter
in pagan beards;

no, but a draught
of red deer's urine
to spike the dew-drops
and elderflower drops.

Behold: an adder
threading the thicket.
All-too-familiar is he.

'A pox and a jinny sting!'
sing the bitter spinsters,
eerie and eldritch,
to the man-blood dusk.

THE ONE RULE IS NEVER TO FALL IN LOVE

In this secret world—caught between the confusions—
my superiors have made me feel too self-important,
underpaid (but with theoretical blank cheque)
in the cosmos within the country within the city.
In the circus of deception the audience faces the tent
applauding the shadows of the acts within the ring
where the lion-tamer is—in fact—a taxidermist
who'll never admit that the lions he tames are stuffed.
The skeleton in my flesh has been somehow turned.
I walk in the public world like a guillotined ghost.
Charm's the veneer. Inside is a tissue of lies
nourished by barium meals and by chickenfeed.

The skeleton in my flesh has been somehow turned...

LILITH

*She is in the form of a beautiful woman from her head to her navel,
but from her navel below she is burning fire*

1

She sees the evil in everyone and smiles
at their backsliding from the Holy One, Blessed be He,
then disappears behind the fruits—her phials
of knowledge—hanging from the Knowledge Tree
and (because she is unknowable) beguiles
the dull, plain, nice, tame and well-known quantities
conscripted by the gallant Samael.
All fell in the fiftieth Hall of Purity
for the Queen of Demons, a honeytrap more vile
than anything Mossad could assign. She
broke the heart of Pardes and won air-miles,
whose trick is simple: to love with brevity,
absconding to the Left Side to face showtrials
where it never parts for her, the Red-damned Sea.

2

From within the depth of the upper Great Abyss
comes the one female, wrapped in a flysheet,
to violate the union of the kiss
dark with the detritus of the high-street
—from public toilets with their public piss
to fast-food joints with their e-numbered meats—
defiling the man and wife whose Eden is
an all-mod-conned and air-conditioned suite,
supergluing glans to clitoris
with a urine/saliva compound she pre-heats,
a bluebottle for her king—Asmodeus—
laying the dirty eggs of his elite...

*Away, away, oh Lilith, release, release
the souls of children from this demon sleet.*

Samael: Angel of Death, consort of Lilith the elder
Pardes: Paradise
Left Side: The Other Side, supernatural source of evil
Asmodeus: Demon King, consort of Lilith the younger

[55]

CANAL (the mirror of simple annihilated souls)

try
when trees are khaki
(in war uniform too)
mirrored
in trenches of canal

and towerblocks are shrouded
in a green gauze
with red cranes erect all about them

hammers and litanies
chain-linking the city
oh the weather as we know it is extinct

try

the canal conveyor-belts itself through locks and
                              traps
its energy
—supercharging the senses—
is an alchemical spray

children cross a bridge

the colour of air is mercury-silver
and great motors growl
loud as dinosaurs along the terrain

in the canal
I am upside-down
and London Zoo
      aviary
is upside-down
      and I
am upside-down
in London Zoo
      aviary

in the cage, in the water
(nothing to do with
the maths of engineers)
labelled as a specimen

try
now
as waterfowl
to love your incarceration

[Author's note: *Le Mirouer des simples ames anienties* was a spiritual text
written by Marguerite Porete, who was burnt as a heretic in 1310]

SAVEJ SINGSING

mi mi savej
bun long nus
mi mi anamol
faea i nius

ae i wael
bus i hot
mi mi stap fiva
gos i flaemaot

kat long dak
fasem nambas
pent long fes
kastom danis

tri i majik
lif i kala
mi sakem spia
mi taetem bonara

yu brekem tabu?
yu gat sem
yu lusum woman
yu lusum nem

spaeda… snek…
flaengfis… hamasak…
hanibi… handredleg…
waelpig… skrabdak…

taem blong hot
taem blong ren
mun i gowe
mun i kambakegen

no jioj! no bang!
no trak! no ofis!
no kot! no mani!
no klos! no polis!

mi mi savej
bun long nus
mi mi anamol
faea i nius

ODE TO THE DOLE (in praise of a free money Europe)
from the Ice Age to the Dole Age there is but one concern
Morrissey

a huge shout echoes through the street like a Red Indian praise song.
the note is sustained, the shout becoming music.
this is not the voice of a line manager. someone is intoxicated...

Original Sin is being born into a society that asks only of its children:
'make money'. thus, our mullahs have decreed. (a crap categorical
imperative). X—we hear—is not complaining, but writing his ode to
the dole, in a red-brick slum of the west. the underclass are the new
aristocracy. they will not lift a finger and dress only in sportswear.
city is their arena. like Ralegh, they deal drugs and write techno-
sonnets, all in towers. they do not need to wade through *Das Kapital*
to know that Marx's adopted country isn't very nice to minimum
wage-slaves. in the new age of Hassan-i-Sabbah, a single joint of
skunk makes you go insane. hashish: the enemy drug-of-choice.
dogs chase the assassins through underground tunnels. beghards!
abraham-men! judeo-apaches! Europe has apologized for colonising
Europeans. somehow, the dole is issued by a Danish/French/
Russian/Greek/German/Belgian king: a begrudging king, a puritan
king, a philistine king, a luxembourgeois king. (admittedly, there's a
million things wrong with our king). yet is he ring-giver. the media
is today what the church was in the Middle Ages: the all-pervasive
brainwash. it brands the psychosphere. Plato's radio, television,
newspapers. advertising is psychic violation. dole is the antidote, a
final overturning of serfdom, a compensation-package for centuries
of oppression. the beneficiaries of the system—a system
that always was/is/will be rigged, by the beneficiaries for the
beneficiaries—were shell-shocked into conscientiousness by WW2.
benefits: for the disabled, the single mother, the schizophrenic,
the redundant. puritans are suspicious of these new timeshare
millionaires who make burnt offerings of charis and black and
sensimilian under the all-seeing eye of the Empress State Building.

X too has joined the underclass (though they think he's beneath them). the cry of gratitude that hurls through the city masonry? it might be his. the exchequer need not worry itself unduly; X is a bargain. verily, free money is economically correct. the hooded child in the tracksuit—the chavi—is a lord of the underclass, his black/white patois the sound of evolution. no one and nothing will convince him that joining the workforce is promotion, not in this christendom, where I sin/ you sin/ he sins/ she sins/ we sin/ you (pl.) sin/ they sin/ it sins etc. call it expenses. Elizabethans walk

with blades

THE STAR CRIED ROSE
after Rimbaud

The star cried rose into the core of your ears.
Infinity rolled white between your neck and thighs.
The sea pearled red onto your crimson breast
and Man has bled black at your sovereign sides.

3

*You want to come back to London? You've no idea how
everyone here will receive you. The look Andrieu and
the others will give us if they see you with me! But whatever
happens I'll be brave. Tell me what you'd prefer. You want to come
back to London for me? What day?*

Rimbaud

LORD FALCONER (song of the raptors)
for Henry Carey, William Shakespeare and Emilia Bassano circa 1590

> *No marvel, an it like your majesty,*
> *My lord protector's hawks do tower so well.*
> *They know their master loves to be aloft*
> *And bear his thoughts above his falcon's pitch.*

in being his raptors we were his imprints
branchers
of the holy garden
hacked back to be forest hawks
none wild—was it Beaudesert?—
we were manned and lured by the masters
and manned and lured and manned and lured
by the whistles of barons
by the eyes of courtiers
and our eyes seeled

we'd be driven in Daimlers in Jaguars
to the tourneys or the colleges
to the elongated tables of Inns of Law
fed-up and feaked and hooded and belled
cameras snatching our souls
from bones
and I hated her then for
and I loved her then for
for our eyes seeled were stars in garters
but calm but calm (as silver)
and the blood-song would build to yarak
to molt
> *to fever*

housed in a mews in London
housed in Charing Cross Mews
jesses on legs jesses on swivels
feeling kind of free in tethers
feeling kind of pampered of important
bating to the panes

I saw your soul across the fen city
talking of ordinary things
in an extraordinary way
talking of common matters
with a royal confidence
in your juvenile plumage
a longwing
I was for your female mantling
film-coveting films-coveting

you beautiful
puking pellets

your gallery of outfits of identities
black-white-black
white-black-white
imprinted with your holy image
I became your imprint

I was given something I could live without
I was given something I would have to give back
was imped was spliced
wishing I had not left my land
for the transit winds
for the international winds
wishing I was no passager
no tercel
two thirds your size

nor booked nor bibled to an ancient system
too far from your sharp-set postmodernism
riding on columns of syllable air
to an academy in the air
                              waiting on
                              waiting on
miles above your master
for lure or quarry to be flung or swung
soaring and stooping openwinged closewinged
ringing up in spirals to a sun-sure pitch
looped to
        God's fist

you saw my vocabulary
my passport
my cap
and saw me comfortable on the padded top
of my block
legs belled
you saw the block
oh
we'd be no cast
literatured in the wars

none tame-wild as you in your yarak moods
none tame-wild as you at your laptop

[Author's note: 'yarak' is an aggressive psychological state characteristic of hawks. It is brought on by eagerness to hunt or by disease. The term is of Persian origin.]

WITTGENSTEIN IN IRELAND
for Karl Johnson

1

This is all I ask of Europe: a simple room
where a hand, god-guided, may be given over to writing
(or drawing a map of the immense topography of mind).
At last, peace in this most wonderful, colourful country
far from disintegrations and putrefactions of Cambridge
on this Western coast where the rock formations are insane.

2

No matter my neighbours—the Mortimers—think me insane,
looming tormented, trance-like, conversing alone in my room.
Why bother explaining the honours and laurels of Cambridge?
Better to sit in a ditch, oblivious, writing
and commune with the true-seeing spirits of the higher country.
A change of aspect is as good as a change of mind.

3

What of Vienna, that necropolis which haunts its own mind,
its spires, its Weiningers, its Trakls, all insane
and broken-spined Austria, shamed, stupid, Satanic country
—the Jews singing Christmas carols in their living rooms—
ignorant of its prophets, the spiritual gift of its writing?
I must say goodbye to Vienna as much as to Cambridge.

4

I shall dictate these notes to some disciple or other in Cambridge.
Publishing: the honorable way of losing one's mind
to fools intoxicated by the historical elixir of writing
(though this writing feels like a man certifying himself insane).
Alone, unless a spirit-light shines into the room,
a man without progeny, property, spouse or country.

5

Of particular interest are the coastal birds of this country:
puffins, terns, curlews, divers, beaked like dons of Cambridge
when Tommy Mullkerrins rows me away from my room.
With its beauty and solitude, Ireland is good for the mind,
though detective fiction—only—keeps me from going insane,
that, and the strange, inexplicable devotion to writing.

6

The psychology of music and humour now infiltrate my writing
as if by the influence of this my adopted country.
Though I worry about going nuts, I'm neither sane nor insane,
and the duty of genius cannot be fulfilled at Cambridge
where technicians and number-crunchers copyright the mind.
God, fill with bravery and inspiration this cottage-room.

Epilogue

I hope they'll allow my insane ghost to haunt Cambridge
for that is the final country, the resting-place of my mind
where the moon prohibits me from writing in my Storey's End room.

BIRMINGHAM
for Zel

1

Sunday in the silver-grey industrial cauldron
an hour to explore
we clambering about slopes
of Hill Street and Station Street
up the piss-soaked steps
to closed malls
closed marts

then trapped in the hygienic heights of 'The Bull Ring'
with an invisible camera crew
you felt the horns and flanks and tail
of a statue of a bull

as across the ether loomed 'The Pallasades'

smells of junkfood and petroleum
in the unmanned city by the unmanned station
as the semi-circular horizon
modelled its finest silver for the fleeting guests
180 degrees of silver / a diadem
mirroring us from New Street
through the glass doors of the ghost-bureau
to cashlinks and departure screens

2

no balance was there in that smoke-screened spaghetti-junctioned
   ski-sloped city!
all was uphill or downhill
or slipping off the edges of superhighways
or falling from ANTI-CLIMB paint signs
onto Japanese fountains
into Chinese markets

lost between the Cathedral and the Cabaret Bar
your cane tapping along the cloud-lit masonry
joining in with the rhythms of the street-corner
where a man—the only man in town—
was crushing tin-cans with a sledgehammer
pummeling them into jagged discs
and tossing them into a brimming bin
he bald, broad-shouldered, self-absorbed
minting his own silver coins

(we christened him Mr. Birmingham)

later as you decoded the art-installation fountains
purpleblue / orangeyellow / pinkred
and how their waterflow was influenced by the wind
my ears were yours

RIMBAUD
following an illicit nocturnal visit to Rimbaud's grave in Charleville in the final winter of 1999

Abyssinia instead of the mind's abyss
dark meat of an African female
businessman cancels the alchemist
Abyssinia instead of the mind's abyss
robed in prose as the camels piss
documents tedious with detail
Abyssinia instead of the mind's abyss
dark meat of an African female

no coat of Bohemia, no lovely lice
no strawberry-nosed goat of lust
Taliesin of France on a dune of sighs
no coat of Bohemia, no lovely lice
the Choan king trades rifles for lies
hyenas and vultures claw the dust
no coat of Bohemia, no lovely lice
no strawberry-nosed goat of lust

instinct of Christ in broken streets
love curdling in Leun'deun squalor
drugged-up, sucking on masculine tits
instinct of Christ in broken streets
redhead Beelzebub groans and bleats
as doctors probe his anal sphincter
instinct of Christ in broken streets
love curdling in Leun'deun squalor

[Author's note: at the inception of this poem I opened my Complete Rimbaud—bibliomantically—at the key poem 'The Stolen Heart', written in the ancient troubadour form of the triolet.]

THE YAWN

The ground opens up its mud-jawed mouth
   yawning a content, self-assured yawn.
      A tree—as if by instinct—adopts the role

of a hand and covers the yawn from the few
   onlookers (myself included). We are
      impressed enough to applaud the good

manners. The ground sighs (as the tree is
   reverting with a machine-like motion to its
      original position): 'You'll have to excuse

me but I *am* frightfully tired.' The fine
   bass tones of the voice are immediately
      winning and everyone seems to know

that it's one of those exhausted nights.
   Even the street-lamps are low in energy,
      half-lit, and not warding off the shadows.

THE PROLETARIANIZATION OF THE BOURGEOISIE

Regularly, in the newspeak of the class-ridden state,
we're informed of an all-encompassing sociological theory:
'The Bourgeoisification of the Proletariat'
i.e. how the galley-slaves these days are happy as Larry,
weighed down with swag, Marx-free, nay, at long last
'indistinguishable' from their middle-class betters
and how all we have to worry about's the underclass
of crims, sluts, schizos, beggars, junkies, poets etc.

Yet all I see's the proletarianization of the bourgeois,
media-brainwashed and work-programmed boot-licks
into computer games, suntans, tracksuits, soap operas,
office parties with strippergrams, cakes like chocolate dicks.
Codes of etiquette are those of the 'tough' not the 'toff'
and *stats* show they increasingly resort to violence:
headbutting, glassing, biting people's earlobes off.
They too are being successfully schooled in the new science.

HYACINTHS

pink light of the pink lanterns
pink dreamachines of winter

purple-blue illumined bulbs
ink-flight mind of cherubs

spinning white into hypnosis
racemes infused with gnoses

bells symmetrical and graphic
ring lyrical and orphic

pink light of the pink lanterns

spring switches off and on
the flickering squills of song

inspiriting bowing vanishing
incense with earth commingling

pink dreamachines of winter

[Author's note: the *dreamachine* was invented by Brion Gysin and Ian Sommerville, a cylinder with slits cut into it, a light-bulb inside it, spinning on a turn-table, an artwork to be viewed with eyes closed.]

EDGELESS

We are protestants, impatient with ourselves, outraged by others,
righteous, we claim a justice that we never yield.

Gillian Rose

let love's risks and labours descriptions of goings-on
in cities in rooms with Abraham Cupid the enigma of confession's
dirty souls in washing-machines turning in their snowflakes
turning and tumble-drying forced back on their own again
                    be edgeless

as from Protestantism to Judaism we flit in light and darkness
for usual manna soup
catching on to lovers who adorn the mask of melancholy science
in this a Roman city (or that an American)
all meeting and connecting numbered among the one
who adorn the mask of gravity in this an English soap
hooking onto professional and all-too-often published thoughts
codes to hang

              like a Jewess in the sands
              exploring a triangle
              wondering at which point
              she'll see the Eye

as from Judaism to Protestantism there's really nothing glamorous
in being who we are—in rooms we searched for—
as parents and meteors (the parents we chose in later life)
vanish into the edgeless black basket of stars
lives empty and tortuous sometimes dismembering Cupid others
neither before nor after crying into flowers our traces and emissions
like grime like gunge our tears of passion bluest veins to kiss

              my being with you
              was / is / will be

                    edgeless

[76]

AL QUDS

So part we sadly in this troublous world,
To meet again in sweet Jerusalem

the winds race north
through the laddered grid
of a suburban street

these are the ladders
I climb at night
but with no ascension

death is young

the winds hurry us

we have many coats

POWERLESS
for Tony Allen

> *We shall be in the service of the most monstrous*
> *industrial and military exploitation.*

after the march on sellotaped streets, I was drained of power and
went to the speakers

fanatics were in evidence   they wore sun-glasses and head-scarves
some carried banners, flags   the Wahibis could hardly say a word
for Xtian saboteurs

then, one shaved like an Egyptian holy-man took my ear   I sat
against a tree still in its childhood, head touching the bark, and
listened to him deny the existence of David and Jesus

the sun sent ministers   I was in their tents   time was in the wind

the voice spoke of Nike—Greek goddess of victory—and how the
sports company of that name had won a mythic victory in the
modern economy

on a silver ladder, the speaker moved his legs at intervals as he
boomed his freethinking ideologies, measured with masterful pauses

I wanted to say that David *had* existed but I was powerless

grass had taken hold   I was buried in wind and light   we who
listened were his wilderness

'enough of the prophetae!' I said, and took my bodymind to the
Great West Road through the incident-tape, machinery, and
fire-smoke-sulphur that made it feel like somewhere between
Israel/Palestine

I went home to my flood-risk area, newly designated and devalued

Gilgamesh was on radio and the rivers rose

ODIN'S SON

in the primitive guts
there are shadows
men
  who
    would
      attack

skull of the moon
in a dark drape
smiles melancholic
up in the canopy

the horns of war
lance again
the ear of peace

no woman to suckle
babies now
who do the fighting

Odin's son
a warrior
 and
  only
    one
      day
        old

PAROLLES (a sonnet)

...only sin
And hellish obstinacy tie thy tongue
That truth should be suspected.

The Shakespearean villain is a perennial. He is our contemporary
even if his cod-piece has evolved into a pair of y-fronts.
Captain Spurio with his cicatrice of sexual frustration and jealousy
bids—in the reptile house of his numbskull—uncoil the pythons
to crush a love he observes, in pain, because he is outside of;
and bids his asps to soft-spokenly slip some venom
in the ear of the female protagonist, and then slide off
to watch the fun (while he's yanking down the zipper of his denims).
All's unwell that ends unwell. He's a modern-day Parolles,
aged courtier of the arts scene, not exactly Mr. Charisma
but skilled at character assassination. He'll blacken the name
of the poet and lover to 'lunatic'. It's everyday life in the polis
for a one-man Reduced Shakespeare Co. exhaling his miasma
  of lies;
and though he eats at McDonald's, he plays a bear-pit game.

OFF-DUTY

The stone paths are soft as carpets.
The sky is two purple curtains.
The night is surrounded by towers.
A drunken man with a black-blue wounded face
is clinging to a silver lamp-post
shining as the blade of a giant bread-knife.
At once I am suspicious.
I suspect him of suffering in public.
He groans as if to confirm the issue.
I memorise his despair.
It is very scenic and the moon is out,
a lightbulb in a white paper sphere.
This is an evening for leniency and a light hand
and thus
                    as an off-duty
                    or irrational
                    or invisible
                    policeman

I patrol the soft paths and bed-like benches
interfering with no one.

VISIONS OF SOPHIA (gardenless)

                                                    in dreams
loon doon
                        black/white   red/blue
the days and weeks   (not years)

        fixation to the gold   in fires of athens
no cars or nothing   no
                        we who need chauffeurs
                                (chauffeuses)
fare-dodging a dance   in   out
                        through   through
                                damn
                                barriers
            tfl
(transport fascists of london)   but all city brings
                                        is visions of sophia
                                        —an eden in eyes—
                                        holding onto life
as falcon   winging
                        through   better way

finding way round barriers   hitting/kicking
                                        (sirens sound her veins)
white in intellectual glory
                        she towers
                                        o
                                new cross
        silhouette taller than any   city

    x-rayed her to the diamond   *centre*
    knowing drink/delusion   (yeh)
    for would mingle shadows
    with her mysterious bird
                                shadow

[82]

the hashish and wine caress
memories in the waterblood
running as rivers intend
to enter the largesse
ie. physics and metaphysics
of a super-body / super-mind
facing down my humility
with a falcon's eye

the male is called 'Assembly'
while the female is called 'Life'
and lo! within her curtains
he'll find his light
the drop!
the drop is falling
and bonds are cut and loosed
from poverty of robbers
to unity
   of rest

following you… your chrism
is no disappointing hour
into the bridal chamber
that reunites the androgynes
aspirant for an equal
dividend of love's gifts
children who beg permission
—so gardenless—
    of ghosts

WHITE SHIP

Stoa ia i no gat kago;
i stap emti, i stap sori
we i no gat kakae o kaliko
be pipol ia i no wari.
'Waet sip i kam!'
Olgeta i singsing.
'Waet sip i karem
evrisamting!'

Man ples i no gat wok.
Hemi storian wetem brata,
i dring bia mo i smok,
i slip long san, i lesbaga.
'Waet sip i kam!'
Olgeta i singsing.
'Waet sip i karem
evrisamting!'

Mama i no gat melek
be ol bebe i no krae.
Sipos yu skwisim woman buluk,
titi blong hem tu i drae.
'Waet sip i kam!'
Olgeta i singsing.
'Waet sip i karem
evrisamting!'

Gavman i no gat plan.
Minista i no gat mani.
Taem oli toktok long paleman
ol bigman i meklaf, i mekfani.
'Waet sip i kam!'
Olgeta i singsing,
'Waet sip i karem
evrisamting!'

Waet sip i kamtru long so
be i stap givim nating finis;
i stilim sendawud, kopra, popo
mo i fulumap net blong fis.
'Waet sip i kam!'
Naoia oli singsing.
'Waet sip i tekem
evrisamting!'

ASTRONOMY

1

40 years of sin
original and unoriginal
40 years of sin
washed down with alcohol

I am surrounded by
the bright and loving eyes of Christians

2

as the streets shrink
and the great monuments
I come into a kingdom
of less than nothing

stars in the pantheon
playing
noughts and crosses

the nihilism and Christianity
I've outgrown

MOON RITUALS
for Harry Fainlight

1
moon in its opening ceremony
    night-clouds
trees are squeaking

2
lamps with periscopic necks
    orange-eyed
bow to passers by

3
the rhythm of the drum
    within
the rhythm of the poem

4
in top-hat and opera-coat
    laden:
bag-man to end all bag-men

5
a helicopter gallops overhead
    moon-horse
neighing war and apocalypse

6
gaunt walls of the hospital
       b/w
a cross-shaped mountain

7
names flash in illuminations
    graphic
neon of Babel flickers

8
in cinema of window
    hissing
a tree is the villain

9
I circumnavigate on foot
    innermost city
complex of psychogeography

10
insect dance of taxis
    beetling
black hoods and bonnets

11
male youth with army-bag
    a conscript
marching into adulthood

12
all low-life in Christendom
    trading tales
for pouches of shekels

13
insults / toxins / *hazchems*
    flushed
into the noxious tunnels

14
Best-Ins and *Supersavers*
    my queen…
it's cheap to feast

15
glorious Os of smoke-ring
    nihilistic
jewels of philosophy

16
a scratch of ignition
    revving
motor gulps the blood

17
spirits of the underworld
    cloven ones
jinns and shaytans

18
rain falls in musical notation
    I revive
to truffling umbrellas

19
brooch holds a green glow
    eye no. 3
pinned to a lapel

20
Cobra Dog and Queen B
    storytelling
to cleanse the infirmities

21
postermobiles flap and swivel
    batlike
in cages of information

22
music of interior pipes
    sonatas
of water and oil

23
people losing to the abyss
    all treasures
ivory combs / tissues of silk

24
red flesh of your nakedness
    expressionist
nude by Schiele

25
curtains bulging with wind
    indoor sails
and the room is at sea

26
ghost-girl sucks a number
    CCTV
films the recycling bins

27
Westway... squares of light
    megalopolis
factories of ideology

28
road-signs to oblivion
    a dead man
drives his own hearse

29
I stand in a kiosk of glass
    primeval
a science fiction unto myself

30
black river / white swans
    joining
in thanks for grace

AT THE YEATS VS. CROWLEY CAFÉ

I trumpet my snot into a non-absorbent napkin
spellbound by the sun
imagining the magic of past/present/future
in a full English breakfast
outside as the silver tables
glow like
　　　　　(scrying mirrors)

> *Yeats is bob-a-job bouncer*
> *at the Isis-Urania Temple*
> *answering to the sobriquet*
> *DEMON EST DEUS INVERSUS*
> *with a professional pugilist*
> *for back-up / alter ego*
> *as Crowley stomps down*
> *the left-hand path*
> *in mask of Osiris*
> *and Scottish mini-skirt*

> *friends come out of the sun*
> *saying: 'we live in the sun'*
> *saying: 'come join us friend*
> *for truly this is the cheese*
> 　　　　　*of the gods'*

but I'm bilocating in a lunar forest
with huge discs chunks slabs of moonlight
like manna on the forest floor
or slabs of chewing gum in the yard
of the DENTYNE factory we robbed as children
—a rites of initiation—
terrified of security guards and guard dogs
or gum laced with rat-poison

ah! friends
the Age of Horus is over

my snot—on the white napkin—
is black with pollution

[Author's note: 36 Blythe Road, Hammersmith, was where the Hermetic Order of the Golden Dawn had their 'Second Order' Isis-Urania Temple and where Yeats and Crowley fought 'The Battle of Blythe Road' in 1900.]

4

The right voice could empty London again…

Yeats

OF CHRIST AND SOPHIA (their emanations)

Son of Man consented with Sophia, his consort, and revealed a great
androgynous light. His male name is designated Saviour, Begetter of
All Things. Her female name is designated All-Begettress Sophia.

1

Christ awakens, pale member in hand, pisses an epiphany,
flushes the banes

Christ limns his film, his pearls of come, to be this font

he's in the ordinary, no mounts

his leprosy is going, he attacks it with files and creams
—religiously—behind the toes

heart blue from breaks, his papier-mâché form is phantom-like,
white as dawn

took a time-machine to New Cross, cursing in the cold,
turning trees upside-down, now from his mouth
to abdomen, he feels the waterfalls, all the wrong emotions,
for Sophia is gone, she in her aeons, in her thirteenth aeon,
evangel of something no one will know, or need to know,
greater than the known

and she is aquiline above her safety-net, loved by the ideas

(her leprosy is cured, first caught from him, who kicked her
in bed with nails like thorns)

Christ in New X, locked in his body, a public toilet

'begat' of Abel/Cain, the 23 daughters, in cauldron of genesis,
born to be Jew, in city of David, waking to authoritarian mornings,
he thinking of Sophia, who flies in silence, better than the sun

thought-matrix, she needs no children

2

in the automaton streets, Christ flaneur

daily they reprimanded him for laziness

Sophia too reprimanded him, in her last judgmentalism,
broke him on wheels, wheels that turn equinoctially
through the historic eras, she smashed his ego, her talons
made ribbons of him, red lines of his mind

she laughed at Essenes, his affiliation with them, called him
a Drug-Vant, thought their texts risible, thought their island
revolution was nothing, laughed at their so-called 'left-hand path',
called him a homosexual

Christ Piscean, lucid-dreaming of crosiers

the shops of Jerusalem, the lost, the humility of the lost,
the tooth-suckers, the hate, the ads, propaganda on the
Western Wall, the Eleusinian malls, the nouveau poor,
how he felt it all, right in his aorta

she never took him seriously when he pointed to the zenith,
her way was academic, nothing could happen on the streets,
the Romans had won, he was living in the past etc.

who did he think he was? Jeremiah? 'the days of the prophets
are numbered' she said (and touched him consolingly)
'Jeremiah's buried in Ireland'

he doubted, his doubt was hers, he drank a beer called
Sun-Dancer, one of her knowers

(her cosmos her superglue)

3

it's Christ's mother's birthday

he calls her from a kiosk, she knows better than to ask him
about Sophia

she hears the answer in his tones anyway: 'I am lame, halt,
blind, withered from her' 'I cannot cure myself' 'your son is ill'
'he is in love'

the virgin on earth is nothing, no longer with Joseph, lives with
a restaurateur

Joseph's on his own, increasingly bitter (usurped by his son,
his god)

Sophia holds the sun as a medicine ball, exercises with it,
is bored of mirabilia… work is her magic

Christ argues with Essenes and doubts the logos… like him,
they have big egos

Christ with government money, Roman discs, he can't afford
to live in an economy

is hipster (knows Marx as hipster) in *Oxfam* robes *traid* sandals

the coins are chewed, the virgin calls back, he stands in the kiosk,
listening to the rings, pretending to be gone

Sophia said to him: 'no woman will live like you'
he said to her: 'I am a woman'

Christ in his tree-house cooks for demons: whore's spaghetti

then he sees them: Ecclesia of the South—the blacks, the students,
the artists, the criminals—riding on flaming horses

Sophia calls the orbs to help her mystery (his mystery)

4

Christ needs to see, not visions

he finds a travelcard, cuts across the city, making a gash in the cynicism/capitalism/conformism of the grid, he surgeon of the cruciform hospitals, for the love she trashed, by night

in tubes of Dis (needs to see her, not emanations)

27, a dangerous age

'abuse, rejection, humiliation, repression… this is love's core'
'the kick in the balls is covenant'
'she is the illuminator'
'she is spiritual consort'

sees David and lions (but she is falcon)

he approaches the house of Sophia, hills he once climbed, doves in his blood

he must see her, she mustn't see him, he in leper robes and tonsured head

Sophia in her planetarium, her dark glass dome, face suffused with light

he sees:

leopards falcons ecclesia jews chocolate factories africas meat pies all the voices soft sounds of animals arks full of animals mesopotamias floods first days and last self-willed and his lion-faced emanations christ carries her recycling human offices human officials mother-machines on and off in the foreign cities they look for love the burn of it in the north cities her feet like birds she tall as light skulls on her dress (knowing death) first bird from ark makes sounds on mountains a woman a jewel aging dying gnostic dawns to nihilist dusks a rented room a red lamp her light's
fate

the temple of jerusalem

is it the black of your jewish hair?
is it the white of your grecian limbs?
is it the blue of your african veins?
no, it is the gold of your inhuman eyes